BOOKS OUT LOUD COLLECTION

VIPs & History Makers

by Grace Hansen & Elizabeth Andrews

BOOKS OUT LOUD COLLECTION

VIPs & History Makers

by Grace Hansen & Elizabeth Andrews

BOOKS OUT LOUD

BLACK STONE PUBLISHING

ABDO

Welcome to BOOKS OUT LOUD!
This one-of-a-kind collection consists of twelve wildly popular Abdo Zoom titles, the bestselling classroom favorites. Get ready to feed your brain with the same amazing Abdo Read-to-Me experience kids know and love at school—and become a powerhouse reader anytime, anywhere.

Please scan the QR code on the back cover to link to the accompanying audio, or visit www.Downpour.com/vips-and-history-makers

Published in 2024 by Blackstone Publishing

Printed in the United States of America

979-8-212-53832-9
Juvenile Nonfiction / Biography & Autobiography / General

Version 1

Blackstone Publishing
31 Mistletoe Rd.
Ashland, OR 97520

www.BlackstonePublishing.com

Contents

Amanda Gorman

Poet & Activist

by Grace Hansen

Photo Credits: Alamy, AP Images, Getty Images, iStock, Panos Pictures, Shutterstock PREMIER

Production Contributors: Teddy Borth, Jennie Forsberg, Grace Hansen
Design Contributors: Candice Keimig, Pakou Moua

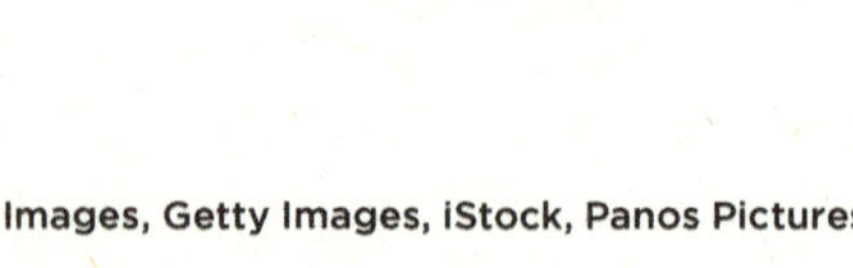

Table of Contents

Early Years

Amanda S. C. Gorman was born on March 7, 1998, in Los Angeles, California.

Amanda and her twin sister Gabrielle were raised by their mother, Joan. Joan was a 6th grade English teacher. Amanda shared her mom's love of reading and writing.

Amanda had a hard time speaking as a child. She worked through it in speech therapy.

Education

Amanda attended New Roads school in Santa Monica through 12th grade. In her senior year, she earned a college scholarship.

Amanda went on to Harvard University in Massachusetts. She studied sociology.

In 2020, Amanda graduated *cum laude*.

Works and Awards

In 2014, Gorman became the first Youth Poet Laureate of Los Angeles. The next year, she published *The One for Whom Food Is Not Enough*. It is a collection of poems about hunger, community, and other important topics.

SHAPING
A SUSTAINABLE
wareness
n dignity,
and equal
nities
FU

In 2017, Amanda was named the first-ever National Youth Poet Laureate. That same year, she read at the Library of Congress. She performed, “In This Place: An American Lyric.” It is about how every person can create change.

On January 20, 2021, Gorman became the sixth and youngest poet to read at a presidential inauguration. At 22, she recited her poem, "The Hill We Climb" for the country.

SEAL OF THE PRESIDENT OF THE UNITED STATES

Gorman added more to her list of works in 2021. One includes a picture book called *Change Sings: A Children's Anthem*. People of all ages can be inspired by Amanda Gorman and her words.

Timeline

1998 — **March 7**
Amanda S. C. Gorman is born in Los Angeles, California.

2014 — Gorman is named the first Youth Poet Laureate of Los Angeles.

2015 — Amanda's first poetry collection, *The One for Whom Food Is Not Enough*, is published.

2017 — Gorman is named the first-ever National Youth Poet Laureate. She is invited to read at the Library of Congress.

2020 — Gorman graduates from Harvard with honors.

2021 — **January 20**
Gorman performs "The Hill We Climb" at the presidential inauguration.

2021 — Amanda publishes more works, including, *The Hill We Climb: Poems* and *Change Sings: A Children's Anthem*.

Glossary

cum laude - a Latin term meaning "with honor" and used to indicate good academic performance.

National Youth Poet Laureate - a title held in the United States by a young person who shows skills in the arts, particularly in poetry and/or spoken word, is a strong leader, and is active in their community.

presidential inauguration - a ceremony to mark the official start of a new four-year term president of the United States.

scholarship - money given to students to help pay for their education.

sociology - the scientific study of human society, like its origins, development, organization, and behavioral patterns.

speech therapy - training to help people with speech and language difficulties to speak more clearly.

Anthony Fauci

Immunologist & COVID-19 Leader

by Grace Hansen

Photo Credits: Alamy, iStock, Seth Poppel/Yearbook Library, Shutterstock
PREMIER

Production Contributors: Teddy Borth, Jennie Forsberg, Grace Hansen
Design Contributors: Candice Keimig, Pakou Moua

Table of Contents

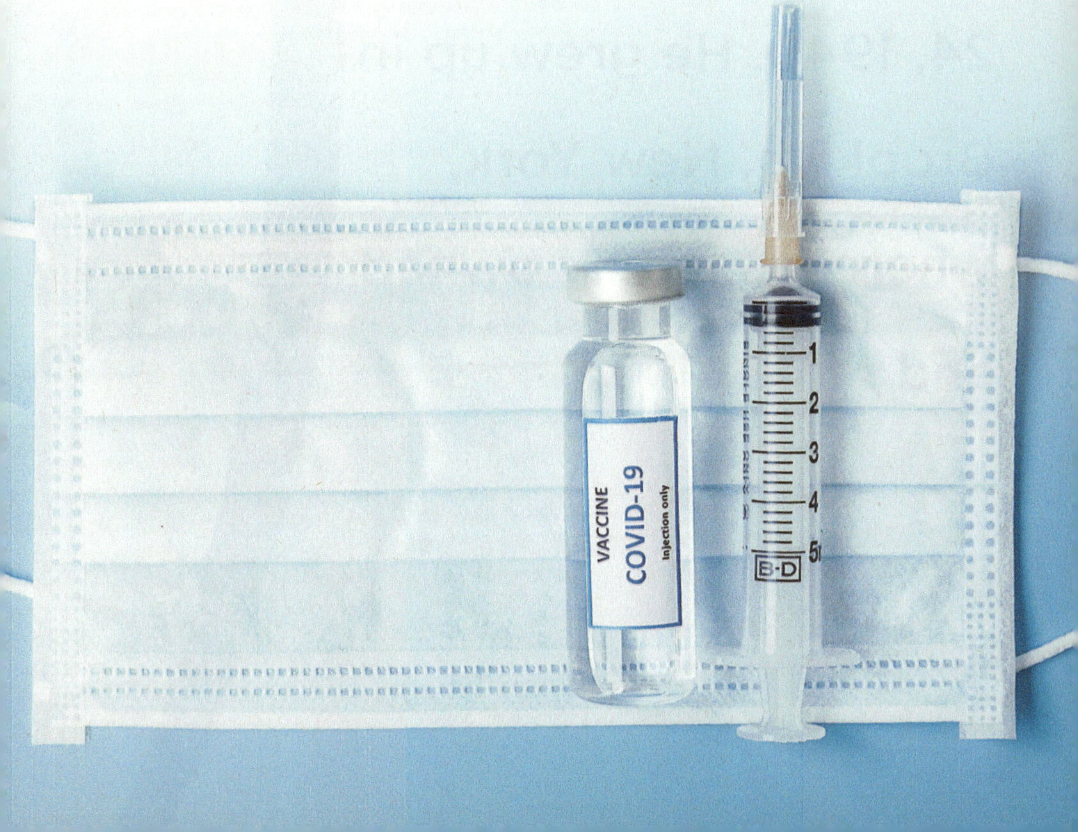

Early Years

Anthony Stephen Fauci was born on December 24, 1940. He grew up in Brooklyn, New York, where his family owned and ran a pharmacy.

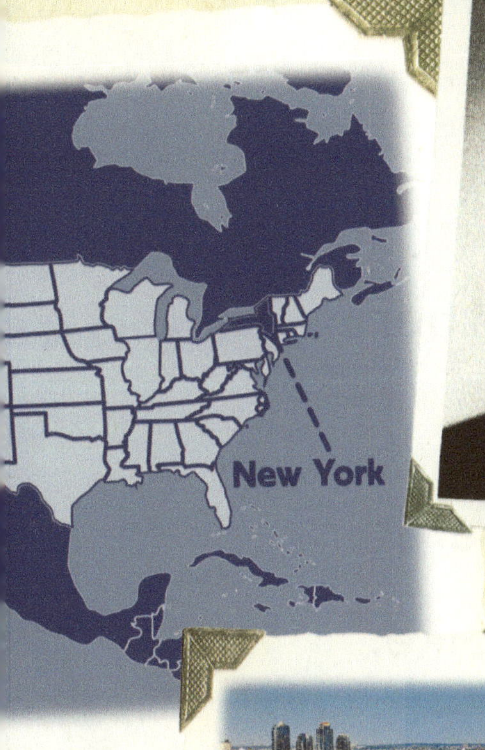
New York

Tony's father was a pharmacist. His mother and sister helped customers. He delivered prescriptions on a bike.

Education

Tony attended Regis High School in Manhattan. He graduated in 1958. He then went to College of the Holy Cross in Massachusetts. During the summers, Tony worked on construction crews.

After college, Fauci went to Cornell University Medical College. He graduated first in his class in 1966. He then trained at New York Hospital.

Career and Achievements

Soon after, Fauci went to work at the National Institute of Allergy and Infectious Disease (NIAID). Its mission is to research, treat, and prevent diseases. In 1980, Fauci became chief of the new Laboratory of Immunoregulation.

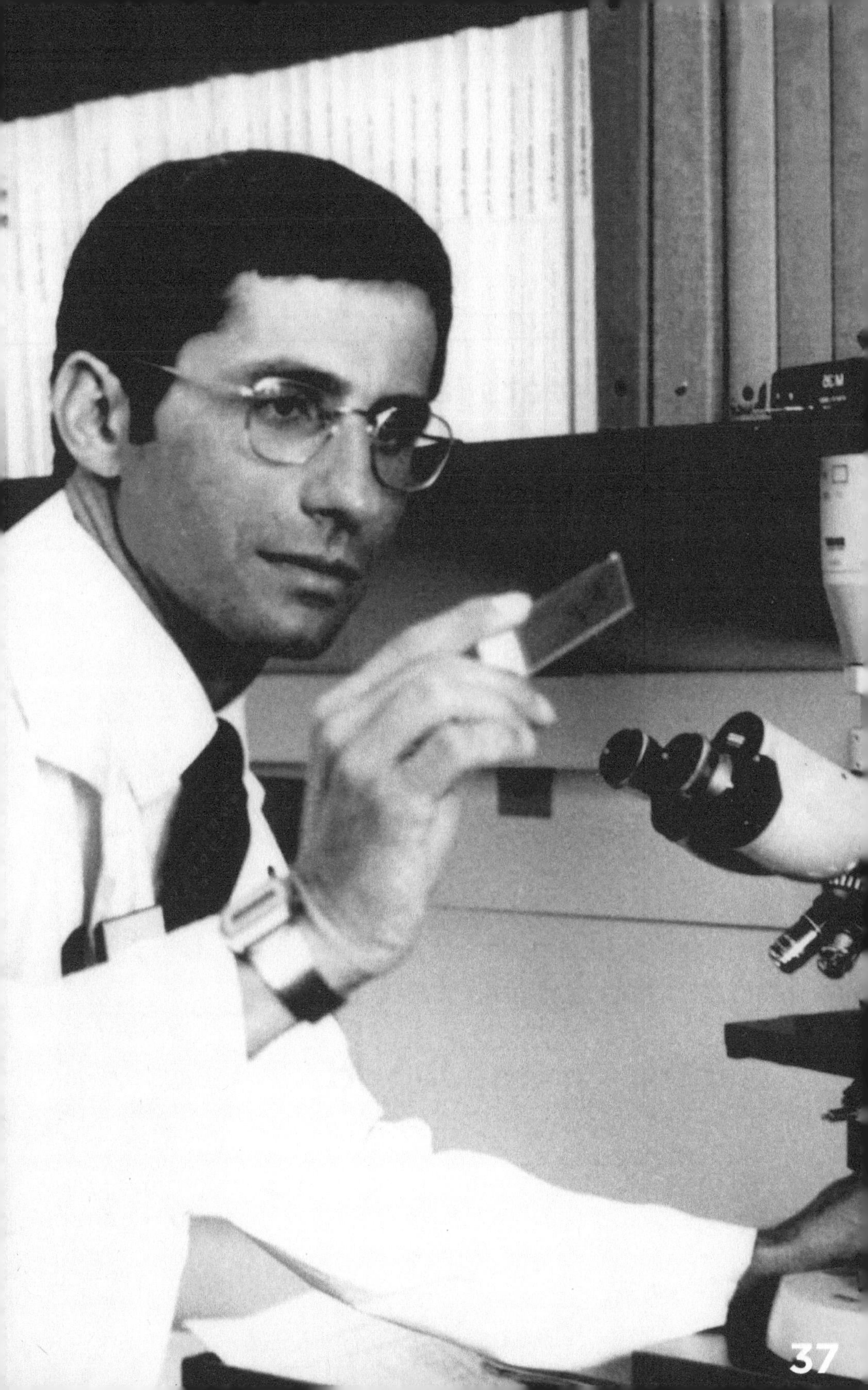

Just four years later, Fauci was promoted to director of the NIAID. He has held this position for many years. His work has made him one of the most respected scientists in the world.

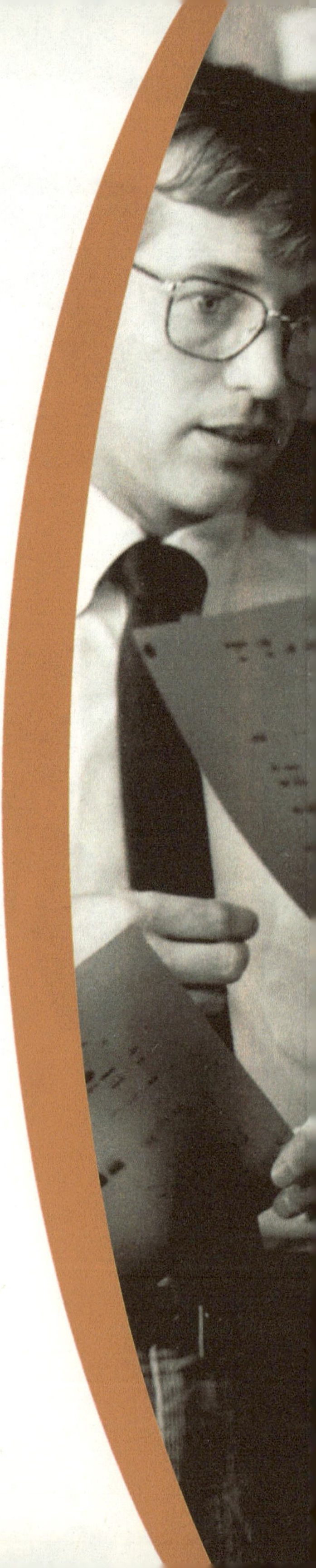

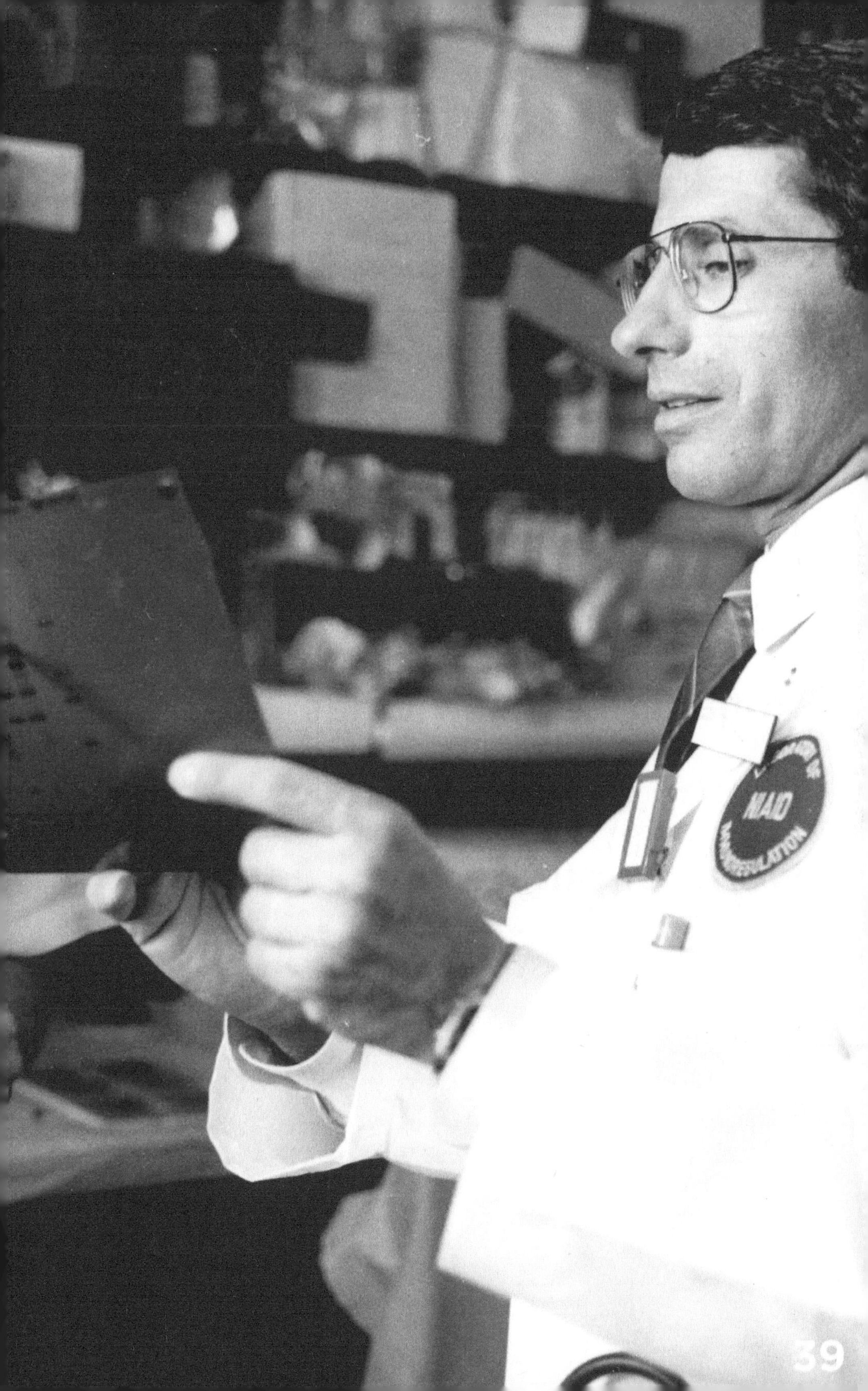

Fauci has helped every US President since Ronald Reagan. He has led the country and world through many health crises.

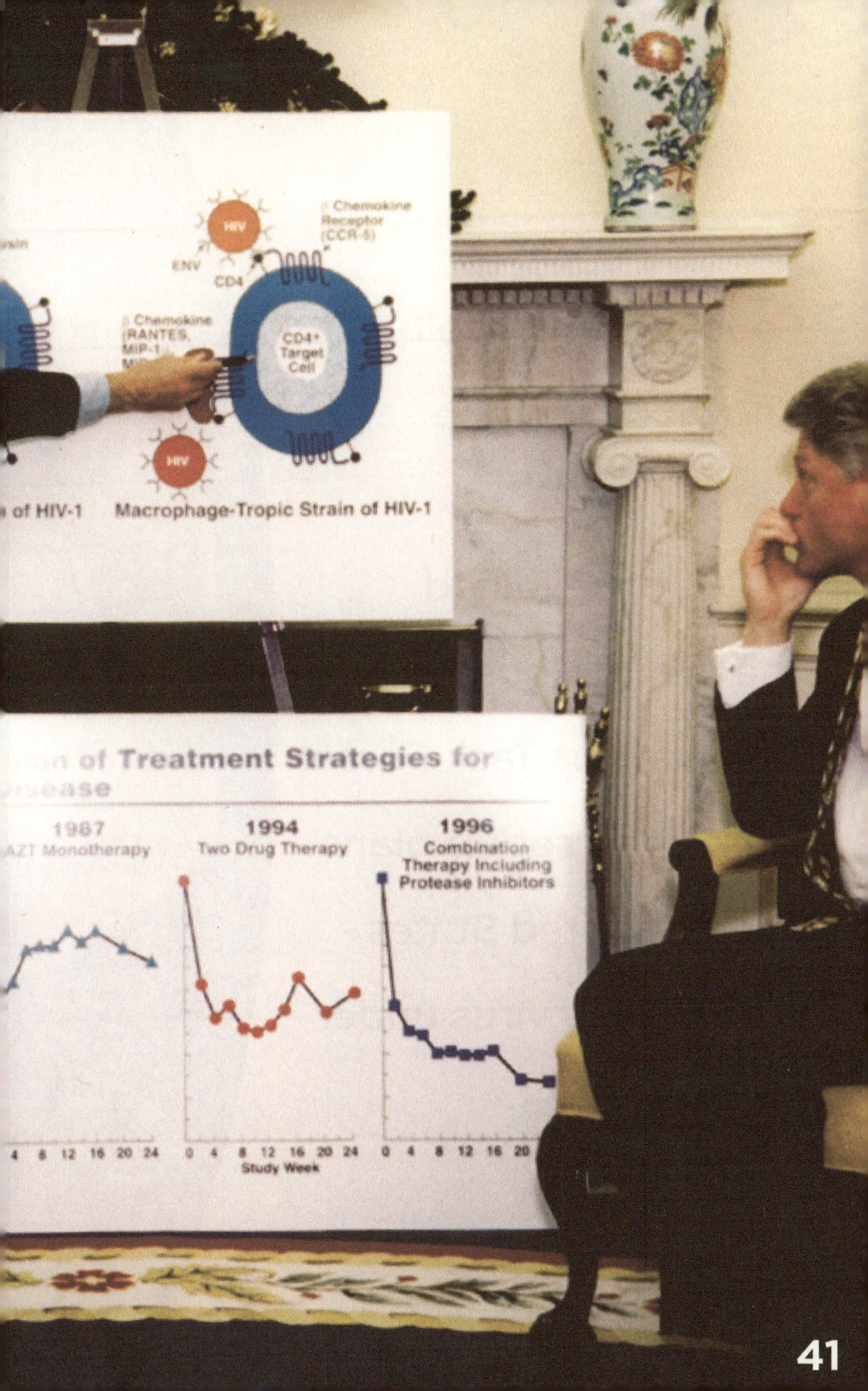
Chemokine Receptor (CCR-5)
HIV
ENV
CD4
Chemokine (RANTES,
CD4+ Target Cell
HIV
Macrophage-Tropic Strain of HIV-1
Treatment Strategies for
1987
Monotherapy
1994
Two Drug Therapy
1996
Combination Therapy Including Protease Inhibitors
4 8 12 16 20 24
0 4 8 12 16 20 24
Study Week
0 4 8 12 16 20

Fauci became well-known during the COVID-19 pandemic. In 2020, he joined the White House Coronavirus Task Force. He helped set up plans for the United States to keep the virus under control.

In January of 2021, Fauci became the chief medical advisor to the president. His experience continued to serve his country well.

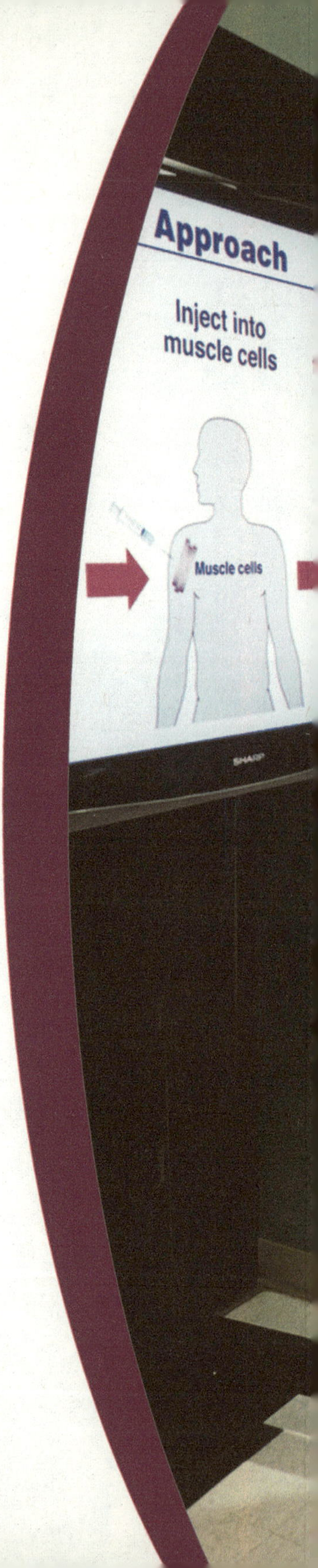

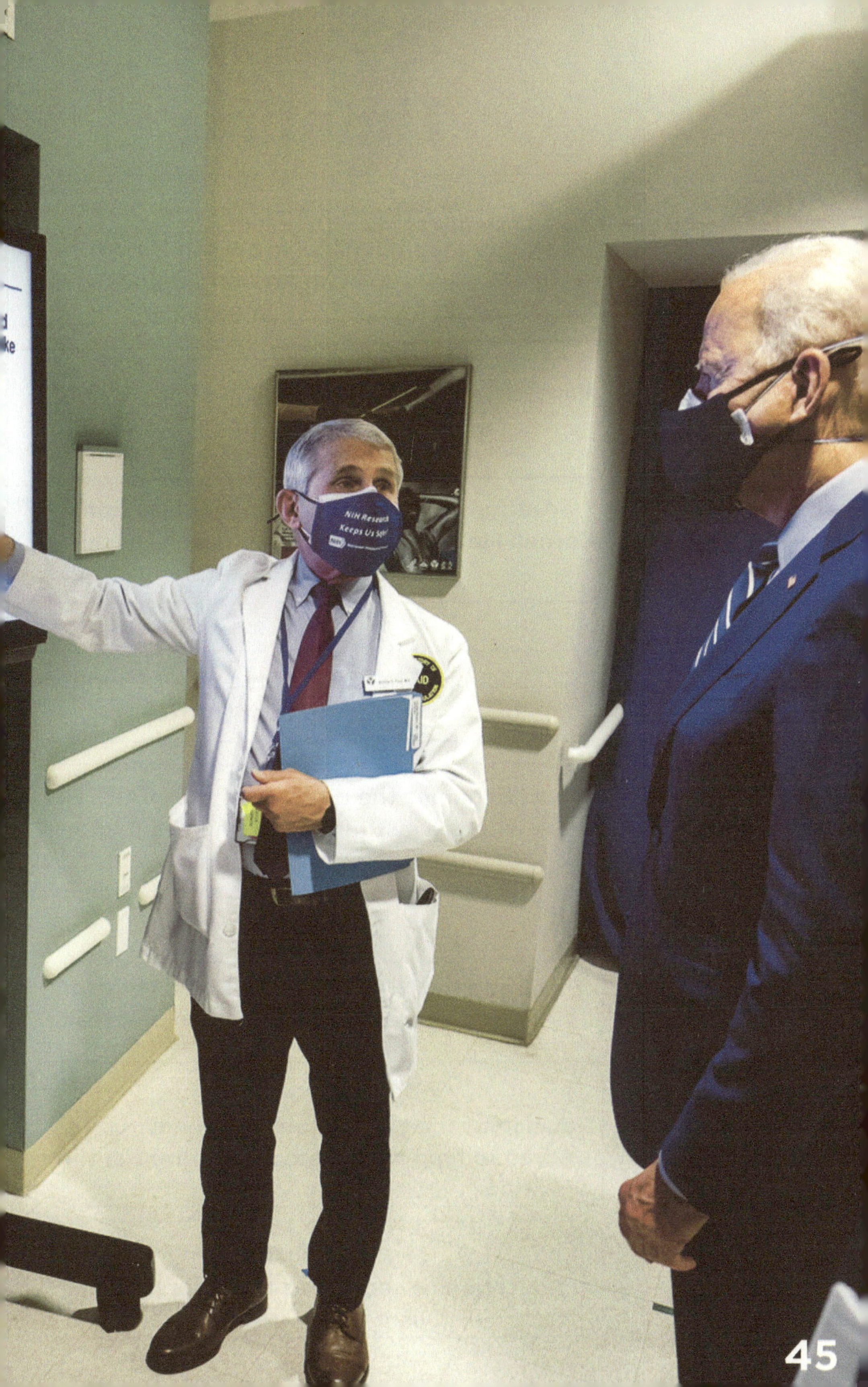

Timeline

1940

December 24

Anthony Stephen Fauci is born in New York City. He grows up in an apartment above his family's pharmacy in Brooklyn.

1958

Fauci graduates from high school and attends college at Holy Cross.

1966

Anthony graduates first in his class from Cornell Medical College. He goes on to train at the New York Hospital.

1980

Fauci becomes the Chief of the new Laboratory of Immunoregulation at the NIAID.

1984

Fauci becomes the director of the NIAID. His work with the institute makes him well-known in the science world.

2014

Fauci and the NIAID research Ebola (a deadly virus) and its treatments during an outbreak.

2020

January

Fauci joins the White House Coronavirus Task Force to help lead the country through the COVID-19 pandemic.

2021

January

Fauci begins serving as the chief medical advisor to the president.

Glossary

COVID-19 - short for Coronavirus Disease 2019, the illness caused by a coronavirus. Common symptoms include fever, cough, and shortness of breath and can be serious for some people.

health crisis - a health situation that affects humans in one or more areas, and generally impacts community health, loss of life, and the economy.

immunoregulation - of or relating to the regulation of the immune system, which is the bodily system that protects the body from illness-causing substances.

mission - for companies, a statement used to explain, in simple terms, its purpose or purposes for being.

pandemic - of a disease, afflicting many individuals over a large area, as a country or the world.

pharmacy - a place in which medical drugs are prepared and sold under the care of a pharmacist.

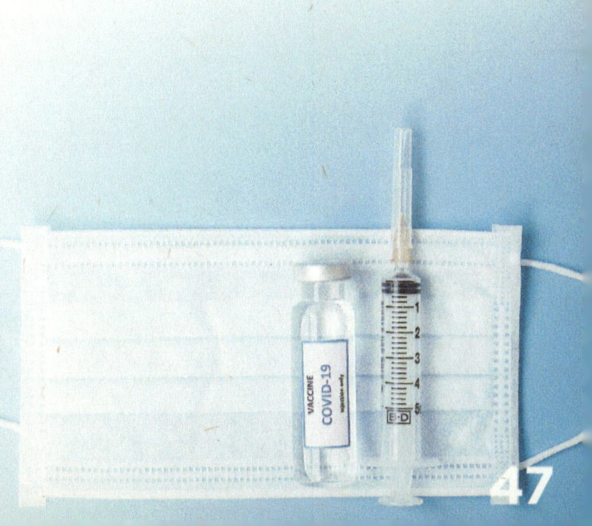

Jill Biden

Educator & First Lady of the United States

by Elizabeth Andrews

Photo Credits: Alamy, AP Images, Getty Images, iStock, Seth Poppel/Yearbook Library, Shutterstock PREMIER

Production Contributors: Teddy Borth, Jennie Forsberg, Grace Hansen
Design Contributors: Candice Keimig, Pakou Moua

Table of Contents

Early Life & Education

Jill Tracy Jacobs was born on June 3, 1951. She grew up with four sisters. The family lived outside of Philadelphia, Pennsylvania.

Pennsylvania

After graduating high school, Jill studied English at the University of Delaware. She continued her education and earned a Doctor of Education in 2007.

BLUE
and
GOLD
UD
TRUE
and
BOLD

The Biden Family

Jill met Senator Joe Biden and his two sons in 1975. Two years later, the couple married. They added a daughter to the family in 1981.

From Second Lady to First Lady

In 2009, Joe became vice president of the United States with President Barack Obama. As Second Lady, Jill focused on things that were important to her, like military families and women's health.

Jill also wanted to follow her passion for education. She traveled around the US to promote community colleges.

In 2019, Joe announced that he was running for president. He won the election in November 2020. Jill became First Lady of the United States on January 20, 2021.

As First Lady, Jill led a program called Joining Forces. It helped take care of military families.

Jill worked hard for teachers and students from inside the White House. It was very important to her that every person gets a good education.

Dr. Jill Biden served her country from outside of the White House too. As First Lady, she continued to teach at a Virginia community college. She was the only First Lady to work a day job while in the White House.

Timeline

1951

June 3

Jill Tracy Jacobs is born. She grows up outside of Philadelphia, Pennsylvania, with her parents and four sisters.

1975

Jill graduates with a Bachelor of Arts in English from the University of Delaware.

1977

June 17

Jill marries Joe Biden.

1981

Jill earns a Master of Education from West Chester. Six years later, she also receives a Master of Arts in English from Villanova University.

1993

After teaching high school for many years, Jill accepts a job teaching English and writing at the Delaware Technical & Community College.

2007

Jill receives her Doctor of Education.

2009

January

Jill Biden becomes the Second Lady of the United States. She focuses on helping the community, especially military families.

2021

January

Jill becomes the First Lady of the United States. She continues teaching English at Northern Virginia Community College.

Glossary

community college - a junior college primarily serving, and often funded, by its local community.

passion - a strong liking for something that one commits time and energy toward.

program - a set of related measures and activities with certain long-term goals.

senator - a member of the Senate. The Senate is one of two houses in the US Congress that has the power to vote on new laws.

John Lewis

Congressman & Civil Rights Activist

by Grace Hansen

Photo Credits: Alamy, Getty Images, iStock, Shutterstock PREMIER, ©Kreeder13 p.5 / CC BY-SA 4.0

Production Contributors: Teddy Borth, Jennie Forsberg, Grace Hansen
Design Contributors: Candice Keimig, Pakou Moua

Table of Contents

Early Life & Education

John Lewis was born on February 21, 1940, near Troy, Alabama. His parents, Eddie and Mae, were sharecroppers. After many years, they eventually had their own land to farm.

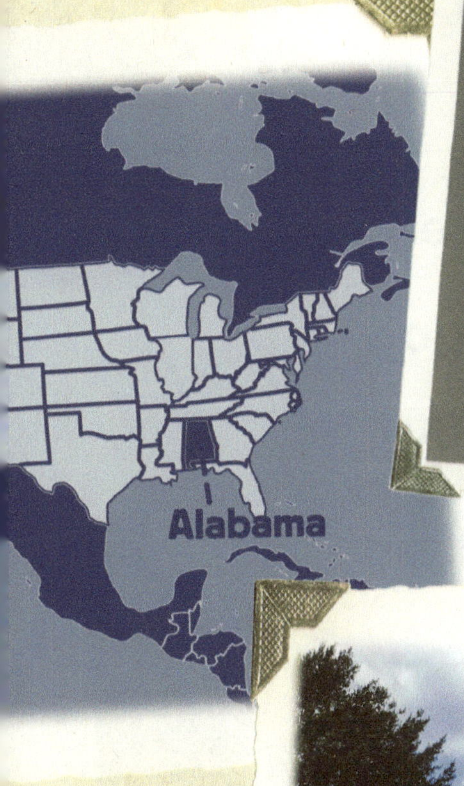
Alabama

STOP

John spent his early years segregated in school and public life. John knew segregation was wrong. His parents asked him not to talk about it with others. They didn't want him to get in trouble or hurt.

POLICE
NG ROOM
HITE ONLY
ORDER
DEPT.

Civil Rights Leader

Lewis was the first person in his family to attend college. He went to Fisk University, in Nashville, Tennessee. He earned a degree in Religion and Philosophy.

In college, he learned about peaceful protests. Lewis was a natural leader. This helped him plan and participate in sit-ins and Freedom Rides.

These events protested segregation laws. And just as his parents thought, Lewis was hurt by people who did not agree with him. But Lewis never became violent himself.

HAISTEN'S
MATTRESS & AWNING COMPANY

In August of 1963, Lewis spoke at the March on Washington. He also helped plan the historic event. He was just 23 years old.

In 1977, President Jimmy Carter asked Lewis to head an agency called ACTION. It helped manage people in the Peace Corps. Then in 1981, Lewis ran for and won a seat on the Atlanta City Council.

US Congressman

In 1986, Lewis again set his sights on the nation's capital. He wanted to make change from the inside. He ran for Congress and won. He served in the House for more than 30 years.

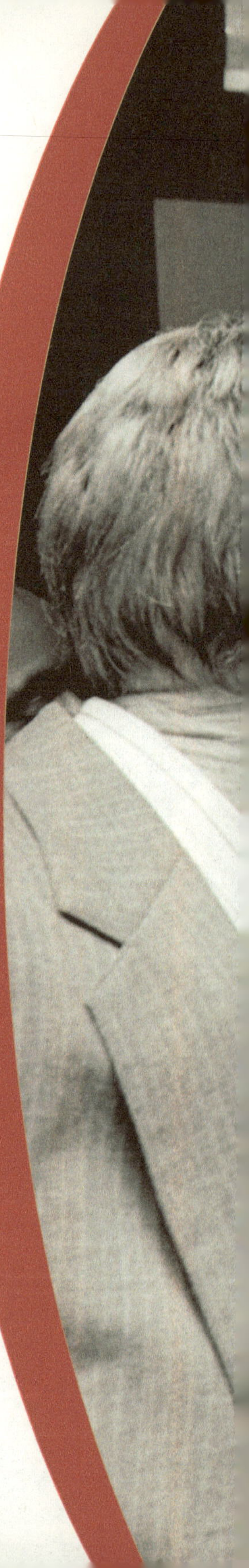

WVEE WAOK
2

Death & Legacy

John Lewis died of cancer on July 17, 2020. Lewis dedicated his life to fighting for civil rights and equality. He is remembered for inspiring change and a better tomorrow.

14 – 10
RIDGE

Timeline

1940
February 21
John Lewis is born near Troy, Alabama.

1959
Lewis participates in workshops on peaceful protesting.

1963
August 28
Lewis speaks at the March on Washington, a historic event he helped plan.

1965
March 7
Lewis and thousands of others protest voting rights in Selma, Alabama. Lewis is badly injured by police in a day remembered as Bloody Sunday.

1981
October 6
Lewis is elected to the Atlanta City Council.

1986
November 4
Lewis is elected to Congress. In his career, he is re-elected 16 times to represent Georgia's 5th District.

2011
Lewis is awarded the Presidential Medal of Freedom.

2020
July 17
Lewis passes away at the age of 80.

Glossary

Congress – the branch of the US government that is elected to make laws. Congress is made up of the Senate and the House of Representatives.

Freedom Ride – any of the bus trips taken by civil rights activists in the 1960s which served to highlight and challenge racial discrimination in the US.

philosophy – the study of the nature of life, truth, knowledge, and other important human matters.

segregation – to unfairly separate people according to groups, especially racial groups. The process of segregating is segregation.

sharecropper – a tenant farmer who gives a portion of his or her crop to the owner of the land as rent.

sit-in – an act of occupying seats in a segregated establishment in organized protest against discrimination.

Kamala Harris
First Female Vice President of the United States

by Grace Hansen

Photo Credits: Alamy, AP Images, iStock, Shutterstock PREMIER, White House

Production Contributors: Teddy Borth, Jennie Forsberg, Grace Hansen
Design Contributors: Candice Keimig, Pakou Moua

Table of Contents

Early Life & Education

Kamala Devi Harris was born on October 20, 1964, in Oakland, California.

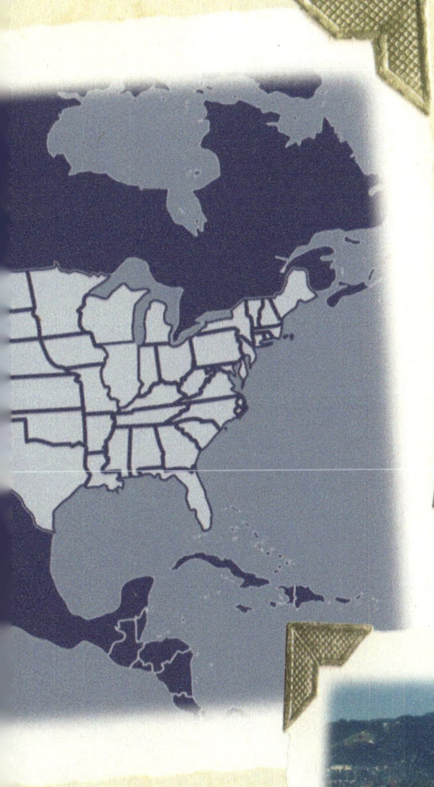

Kamala's family lived in Berkeley, California. Her father, Donald, is Jamaican. He was a professor. Shyamala, her mother, was from India. She was a scientist.

When Kamala was 12, her parents divorced. She and her younger sister Maya moved with their mother to Quebec, Canada. There, Kamala finished middle school and high school.

In 1982, Kamala left for Washington, DC to attend college at Howard University. She then returned to California for law school. She graduated in 1989.

BOLAND
BOLAND

Career

Harris's first job was as a deputy district attorney. In 1998, she went to work with the San Francisco District Attorney's Office. In 2004, her hard work led to her becoming district attorney of San Francisco.

FOR JUSTICE
DISTRICT ATT

In 2010, Harris was elected attorney general of California. She was the first female and Black person to earn the job!

FORNIA REP

In 2015, Kamala decided to run for Senate. Harris earned many votes and easily won the election. She took office as a United States senator in 2017.

KAMALA

In 2019, Kamala announced she would run for president of the United States. She later dropped out of the race. It wasn't long before Joe Biden asked Harris to be his running mate.

The First but Not the Last

In November of 2020, Harris was elected the first female vice president of the United States. She took office in January of 2021. She said, "While I may be the first woman in this office, I will not be the last."

Timeline

1964

October 20
Kamala Devi Harris is born in Oakland, California.

1986

Harris graduates from Harvard University with a degree in political science and economics.

1989

Harris graduates from University of California, Hastings College of Law.

1990

Harris is hired as deputy district attorney in Alameda County, CA.

2004

Harris takes office as the district attorney of San Francisco.

2011

Harris takes office as the first female and first Black attorney general of California.

2017

January 3
Kamala joins the United States Senate.

2021

January 20
Kamala Harris becomes the first female vice president of the United States.

Glossary

attorney general – the principal legal officer who represents a country or state in legal proceedings and gives legal advice to the government.

district attorney – a public official who acts as prosecutor for the state or the federal government in court in a particular district.

elected – chosen by means of voting.

running mate – an election candidate for the lesser of two closely related political offices, for instance, a person running for president chooses a running mate who will become vice president.

Senate – one of the two houses of the United States Congress whose responsibilities include all lawmaking within the country.

Tom Brady

NFL Great and Super Bowl MVP

by Grace Hansen

Photo Credits: Alamy, AP Images, Getty Images, Icon Sportswire, iStock, Shutterstock PREMIER

Production Contributors: Teddy Borth, Jennie Forsberg, Grace Hansen
Design Contributors: Candice Keimig, Pakou Moua

Table of Contents

Early Life & Education

Thomas Edward Patrick Brady Jr. was born on August 3, 1977. He grew up in San Mateo, California, with three older sisters.

Tom loved football from a young age. In high school, he was a star baseball and football player. After graduating in 1995, Tom was asked to play for a pro baseball team. But he said no. He had other plans.

The 1995 All-CCS Baseball Team

Tom put together a highlight reel of his high school games. He sent it to big football colleges. The Michigan Wolverines asked Brady to play for them.

NFL Pro

NFL scouts did not show much interest in Brady. Some thought he was too slow. But Brady still got a call during the 2000 NFL Draft. It was from the New England Patriots.

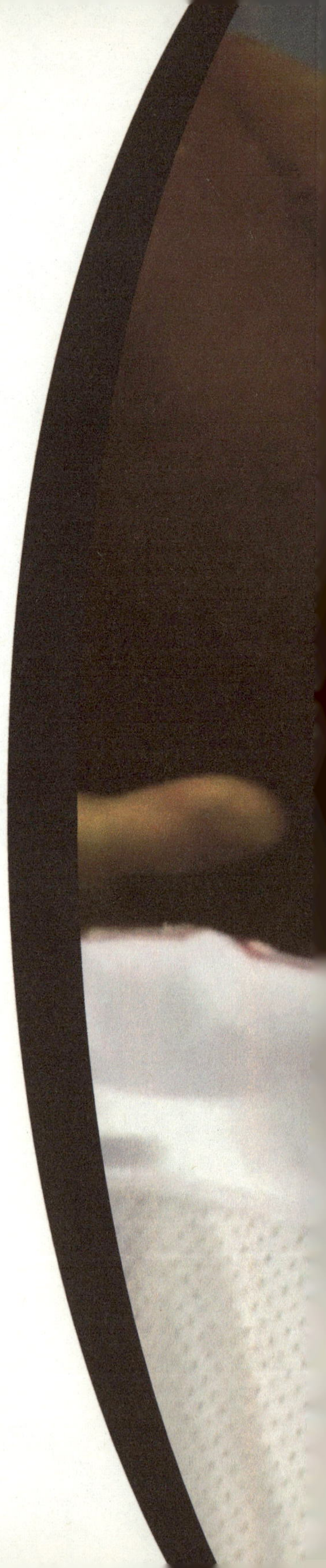

PATRIOTS

Brady rarely played in his rookie year. Then quarterback Drew Bledsoe got hurt early in the 2001 season. Brady won his first game as starting quarterback on September 30th. He ended that season as the Super Bowl MVP!

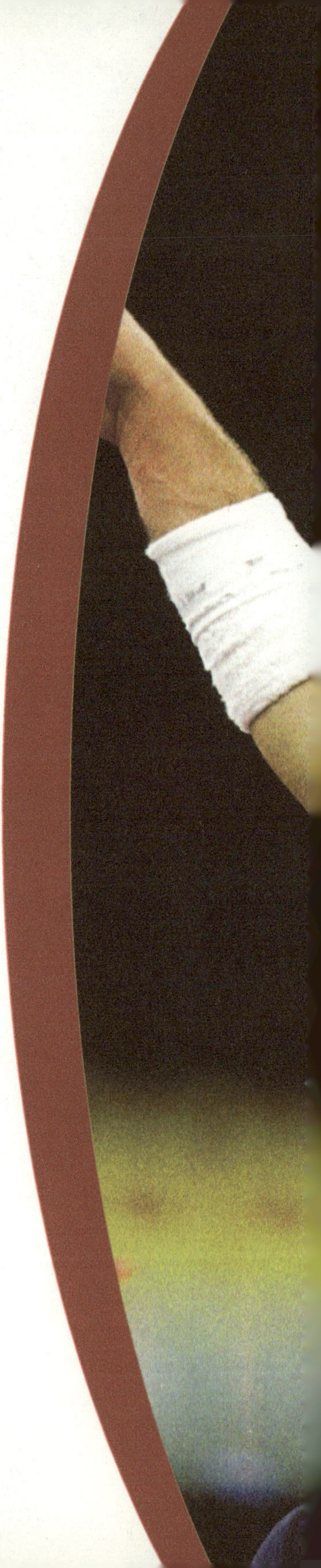

By 2005, Brady had led the Patriots to three Super Bowl wins. In the 2007 regular season, Brady threw 50 touchdown passes. And the Patriots topped it off with a perfect 16-0 record.

By 2019, Brady and the Patriots had collected three more Super Bowl rings. Then after 20 years with New England, Brady signed with the Tampa Bay Buccaneers in March of 2020.

TAMPA BAY
BUCCANEERS

New Team, Same Tom

The Buccaneers had some winning seasons before Brady. But the quarterback brought a whole new energy to Tampa Bay. That season, the team clinched their first playoff berth since 2007.

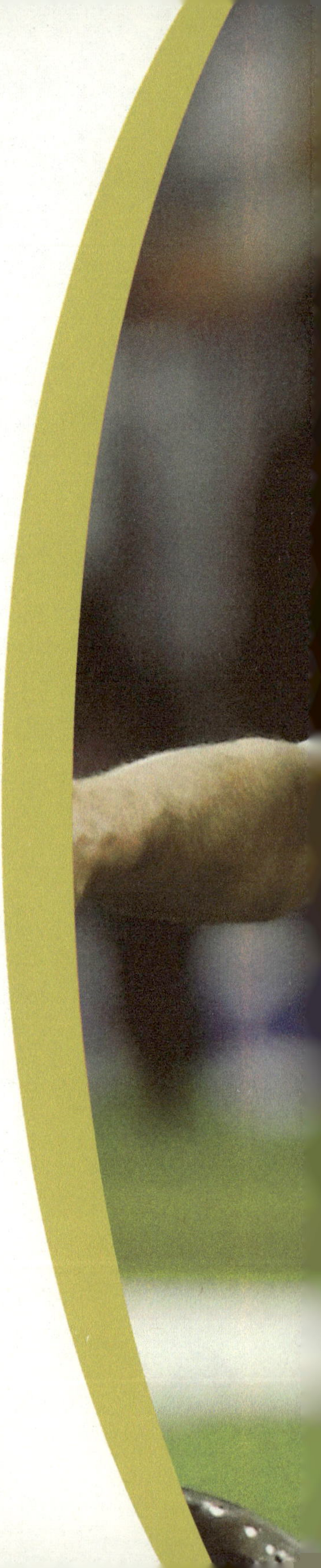

Brady then led the Buccaneers all the way to Super Bowl LV. On February 7, 2021, Tampa Bay defeated the Kansas City Chiefs 31-9. Brady was named Super Bowl MVP for a record fifth time. The NFL great is sure to excite fans for years to come.

Timeline

1977 **August 3**
Thomas Edward Patrick Brady Jr. is born in California.

1995 Tom graduates from high school. He goes on to attend the University of Michigan and plays QB for the Wolverines.

2000 The NFL's New England Patriots pick Tom Brady in the draft. He starts his career as a fourth string QB.

2001 **September 30**
Brady plays and wins his first game as starting quarterback.

2002 Brady and the Patriots win Super Bowl XXXVI after the 2001 NFL season.

2020 After 20 seasons and an incredible six Super Bowl wins with the Patriots, Brady joins the Tampa Bay Buccaneers.

2021 **February 7**
After his first season with the Buccaneers, Brady brings a Super Bowl win to Tampa Bay. It is Brady's seventh Super Bowl win.

Glossary

draft – the choosing of one or more people for sports teams.

highlight reel – the best moments caught on video in one's sports career put together to create one film.

MVP – short for "Most Valuable Player," an award given to a player who, overall, performed the best in a game or series.

playoff berth – when a position in the playoffs is secured ahead of the regular season's conclusion.

pro – short for professional.

scout – a person who looks for new sports talent.

Amelia Earhart

Aviation Pioneer

by Grace Hansen

Photo Credits: Ames Historical Society, AP Images, Corbis, Getty Images, iStock, Shutterstock, © User:Hellerick / CC-SA-3.0 p.19

Production Contributors: Teddy Borth, Jennie Forsberg, Grace Hansen
Design Contributors: Laura Mitchell, Dorothy Toth

Table of Contents

Early Life

Amelia Mary Earhart was born on July 24, 1897. She was born in Atchison, Kansas.

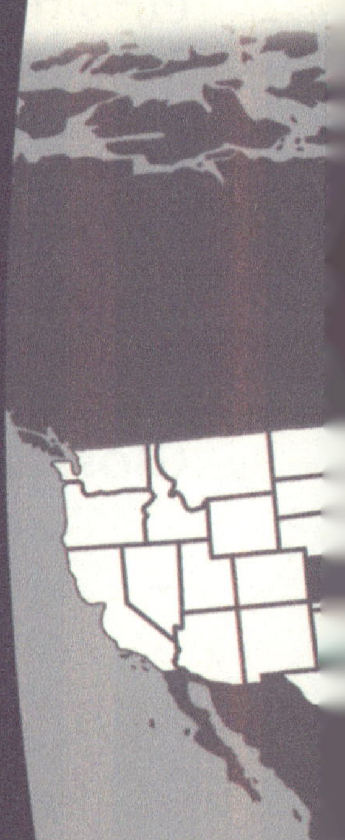

Frank Hawks was a famous aviator. In 1920, he took Amelia on her first plane ride. She loved it!

Up, Up, and Away!

Amelia's interest in flying grew. She took flying lessons. She even bought a plane. She named it *The Canary*. It was bright yellow.

AIRPO

In 1928, Amelia was invited on a flight. The flight crossed the Atlantic Ocean. She was the first woman to do this.

The flight made Amelia famous. But she was only a passenger. She wanted to make the trip on her own. So, on May 20, 1932, she did!

Next, Amelia flew across the Pacific Ocean. Now she was ready for a greater challenge. She wanted to fly around the world! The flight would start in California.

Amelia and navigator Fred Noonan took off from Miami, Florida, on June 1, 1937. Amelia completed about 22,000 miles (35,400 km) of her trip. She had about 7,000 miles (11,300 km) to go.

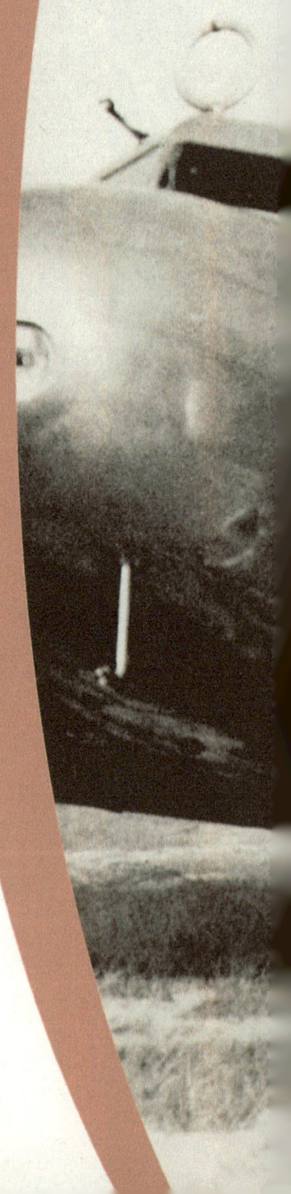

Missing

On July 2, The US Coast Guard waited near a small island in the Pacific. Amelia was supposed to refuel there. She never made it. Amelia and her plane have never been found.

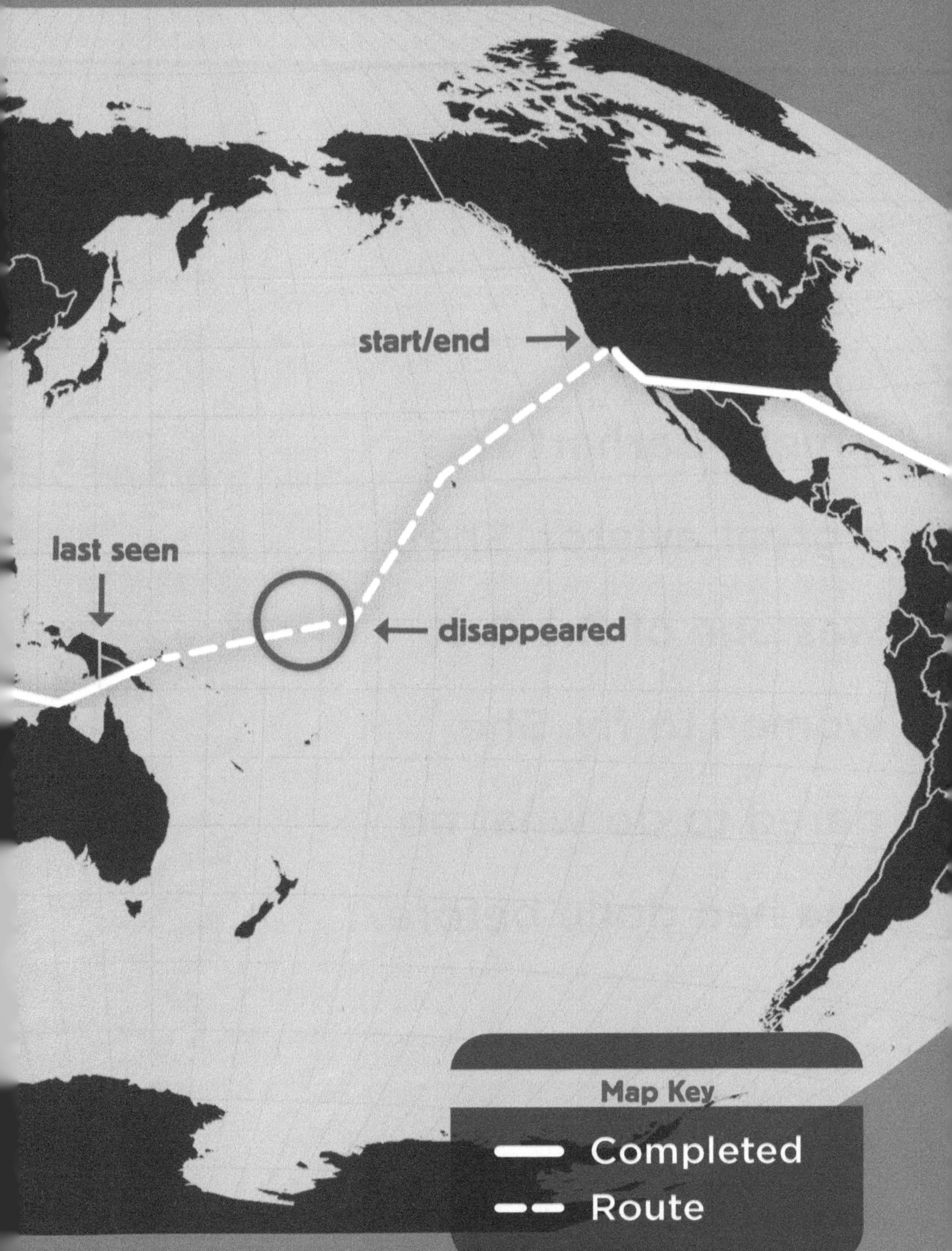
start/end
last seen
disappeared
Map Key
Completed
Route

Legacy

Amelia Earhart was a great aviator. She was one of the first women to fly. She dared to do what no one had done before.

Timeline

1897

July 24
Amelia Mary Earhart is born in Atchison, Kansas.

1920

December 28
Amelia takes her first airplane ride with pilot Frank Hawks.

1921

January 3
Amelia takes her first flying lesson. She saves money for a plane, *The Canary*.

1928

June 17–18
Amelia is the first female passenger on a trans-Atlantic flight.

1932

May 20–21
Amelia flies solo across the Atlantic. She is the first woman to do so.

1937

June 1
Amelia departs from Miami on her flight around the world.

July 2
Amelia goes missing somewhere in the Pacific Ocean.

Glossary

challenge – something that is hard to do.

navigator – a person who is skilled at directing an aircraft on the right course.

passenger – a person riding in a vehicle.

Cesar Chavez

Latino American Civil Rights Activist

by Grace Hansen

Photo Credits: AP Images, Cesar Chavez Foundation, Corbis, Getty Images, iStock, Shutterstock

Production Contributors: Teddy Borth, Jennie Forsberg, Grace Hansen
Design Contributors: Laura Mitchell, Dorothy Toth

Table of Contents

Early Life

Cesar Chavez was born on March 31, 1927. He grew up near Yuma, Arizona. His family had a farm.

Arizona

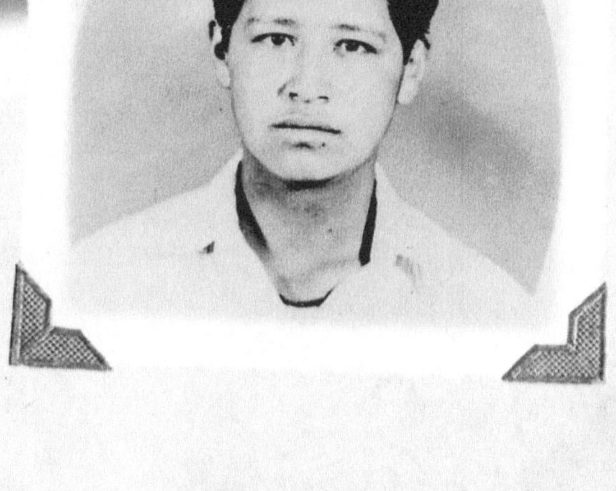

Cesar's parents were from Mexico. They came to the United States before he was born. They taught him to help the less fortunate.

Cesar's family lost their farm when he was 11. They moved to California for work. They became migrant farmworkers.

Taking a Stand

Farmwork was very hard. Workers had long hours. They were paid very little. They did not get breaks or clean water.

Farmworkers needed rights. Cesar's dream was to set up a union. This union would protect farmworkers.

In 1952, Cesar got a great job. This job let him help immigrants. He was happy with his work. But he still wanted to help farmworkers.

In 1962, Cesar started the National Farm Workers Association (NFWA). It asked farm owners to make better working conditions. Many refused. Cesar used boycotts and protests to make change happen.

Years later, Cesar was seeing progress. Farmworkers were getting fairer treatment. They got breaks and clean water. They had better pay and much more.

Death & Legacy

Cesar spent his life helping the poorest people. He taught farmworkers about their rights. And he worked hard to get them those rights. He died on April 23, 1993.

Timeline

1927 **March 31**
Cesar Estrada Chavez is born in San Luis, Arizona.

1938 The Chavez family loses their farm. They move to California to work as migrant farmers.

1948 Cesar marries Helen Fabela. They go on to have 8 children.

1952 Chavez gets a job helping Latinos become citizens and vote.

1962 Chavez starts the NFWA. It is later called the United Farm Workers of America (UFW).

1967 The first of three UFW grape boycotts begins to call attention to unfair conditions.

1980s Around 45,000 farmworkers are protected by contracts to ensure fair treatment.

1993 **April 23**
Cesar dies in Arizona. The Cesar E. Chavez Foundation is founded.

Glossary

boycott – an act of joining with others to ban a certain person, product, place, or organization.

fortunate – lucky.

immigrant – a person who moves to a new country to live.

migrant – a person who moves from place to place to find work.

union – an organized group of workers who come together to impact their wages, hours, health, safety, and other work-related issues.

Eleanor Roosevelt

First Lady & Equal Rights Advocate

by Grace Hansen

Photo Credits: AP Images, Corbis, Getty Images, iStock, Shutterstock

Production Contributors: Teddy Borth, Jennie Forsberg, Grace Hansen
Design Contributors: Laura Mitchell, Dorothy Toth

Table of Contents

Early Life

Anna Eleanor Roosevelt was born on October 11, 1884. She grew up in New York City, New York.

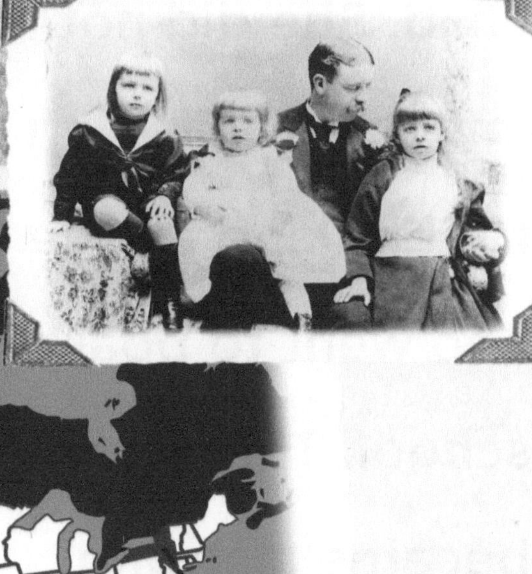

New York

Eleanor was a shy child. She did not feel important. She left for England at age 15. She went to boarding school. There, she became a strong person.

Eleanor returned home ready to make a difference. She started work at a settlement house. She taught immigrant children.

In 1902, Eleanor met Franklin Roosevelt. They married on March 17, 1905. They had six children.

Making a Difference

In 1933, Franklin became the 32nd president. This made Eleanor the First Lady. She used her title to help many people.

Franklin had been sick for many years. Traveling was hard for him. So Eleanor often traveled for him. She met people all over the country. She learned about their problems.

Eleanor knew what it was like to feel weak. So she spoke for people who were treated unfairly. She helped American workers and the poor. She helped women and African Americans.

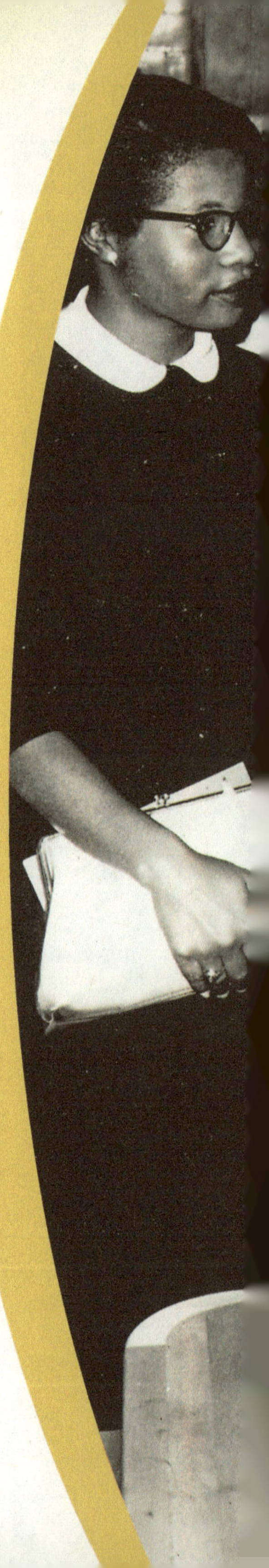

In 1946, Eleanor was elected to the United Nations. Her focus was on human rights. Now she could help people around the world.

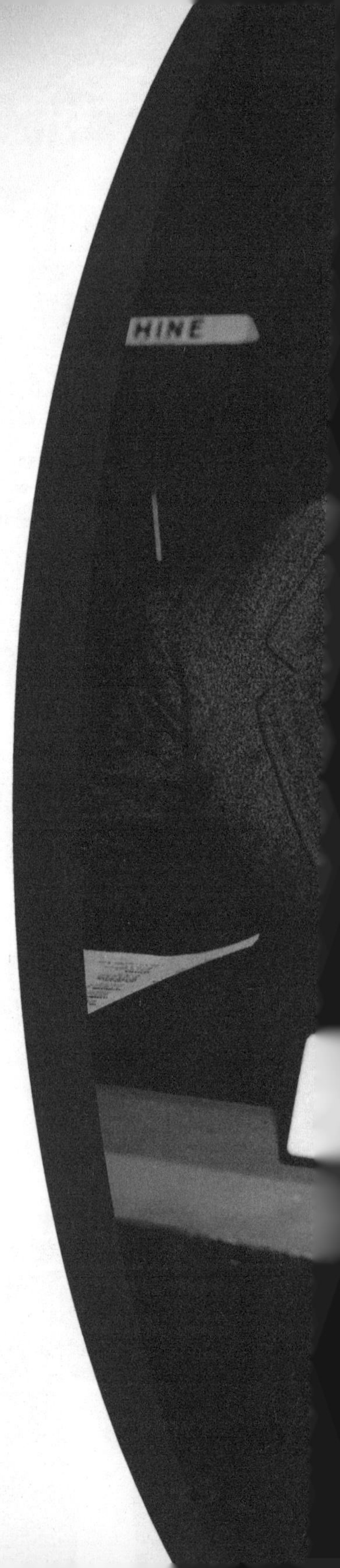

CANADA
TS-UNIS D'AMÉRIQUE

Death & Legacy

Eleanor forever changed the role of the First Lady. She worked to do what was right and good. She died on November 7, 1962.

THE UNIVERSAL DECLARAT
OF Human Rights

Timeline

1884

October 11

Anna Eleanor Roosevelt is born in New York City, New York.

1905

March 17

Eleanor marries Franklin D. Roosevelt.

1920

Eleanor joins the League of Women Voters. Women get the right to vote later that year.

1933

Eleanor becomes the First Lady ofthe United States.

1934

Eleanor begins work with the NAACP to help in the fight for equality.

1946

Eleanor is elected to the United Nations as the head of the Human Rights Commission.

1962

November 7

Eleanor dies at the age of 78.

Glossary

First Lady – the wife of the chief executive of a country.

immigrant – a person who moves from one country to another to live.

NAACP – stands for the National Association for the Advancement of Colored People. The organization formed in 1909 to ensure equality of rights of all persons, and to end racism.

settlement house – a place that provides community services to people in a crowded part of a city.

United Nations – a group made up of most of the world's countries. It was created in 1945 to promote peace, security, and unity.

Ella Fitzgerald

American Jazz Singer

by Grace Hansen

Photo Credits: AP Images, Corbis, Getty Images, iStock, Library of Congress, Shutterstock,©Carl Van Vechten p.5

Production Contributors: Teddy Borth, Jennie Forsberg, Grace Hansen
Design Contributors: Laura Mitchell, Dorothy Toth

Table of Contents

Birth & Early Life

Ella Fitzgerald was born on April 25, 1917. She was born in Newport News, Virginia.

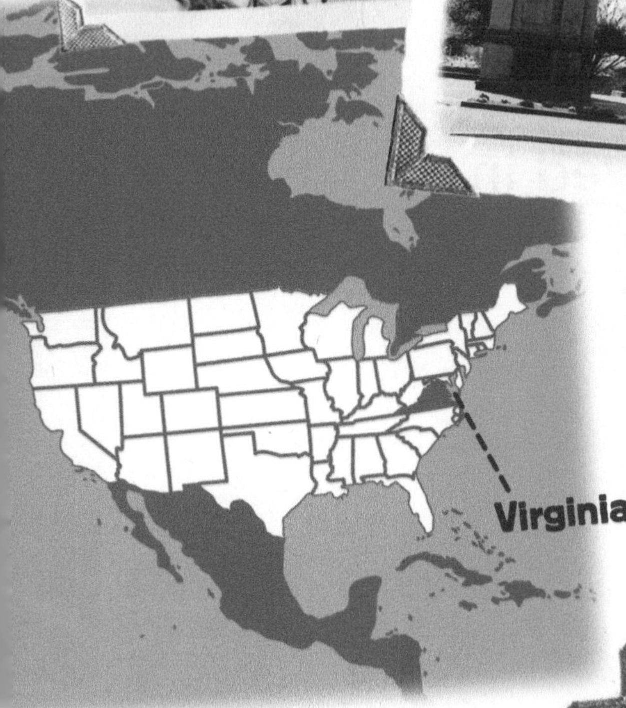
Virginia

Ella's family moved to Yonkers, New York. Ella's mother died in 1932. She moved in with her aunt.

The Apollo

By 1934, Ella was living on the streets. She entered a contest at Harlem's Apollo Theater. She hoped to win the prize money. She sang two songs.

The audience loved Ella. So, she entered many more talent shows. And she kept winning!

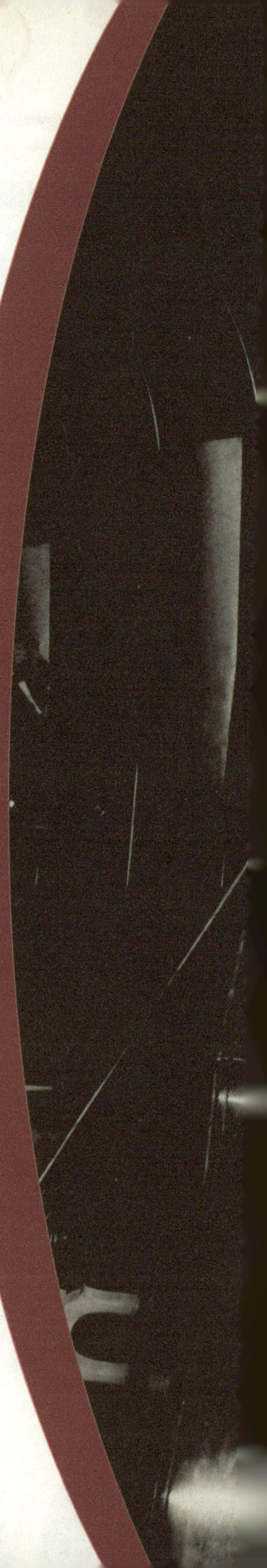

In 1935, Ella recorded her first song. It was called, "Love and Kisses." She was also performing at the Savoy. It was a famous ballroom.

Fame!

In 1938, Ella recorded "A-Tisket, A-Tasket." It was very popular. It sold 1 million copies! Ella was famous.

The 1950s and 1960s were great for Ella. She made very popular music. The very first Grammy Awards was held in 1958. Ella won two Grammys!

Ella went on to win 13 Grammys. She recorded over 200 albums and 2,000 songs! She won many other awards. She also gave a lot to charity.

Death & Legacy

On June 15, 1996, Ella died. She was at her home in Beverly Hills, California. She is remembered as "The First Lady of Song."

Timeline

1917

April 25
Ella Jane Fitzgerald is born in Newport News, VA. Soon after, Ella and her mother move to Yonkers, NY.

1932

Ella's mother dies. Ella moves in with her aunt.

1934

Ella is living on the streets. She enters a contest at the Apollo Theater. She wins first place.

1935

Ella records "Love and Kisses." She is performing regularly at the Savoy.

1938

Ella records her first number one song "A-Tisket, A-Tasket."

1958

Ella wins two Grammys at the first ever Grammy Awards.

1970s

Ella is performing concerts around the world.

1996

June 15
Ella dies in Beverly Hills, CA.

Glossary

charity - generous donations and actions to aid the poor or ill.

contest - a competition for a prize.

famous - well-known by many people for something you do.

Grammy - a statue awarded by the National Academy of Recording Arts and Sciences for outstanding achievement.

talent - a unique and natural ability.

Harry Houdini

Illusionist & Stunt Performer

by Grace Hansen

Photo Credits: Corbis, Getty Images, iStock, Library of Congress, Shutterstock, ©Harvard Theatre Collection, Houghton Library p.5, ©User:rcade / CC-SA-2.0 p.7

Production Contributors: Teddy Borth, Jennie Forsberg, Grace Hansen
Design Contributors: Laura Mitchell, Dorothy Toth

Table of Contents

Birth

Erik Weisz was born on March 24, 1874. He was born in Budapest, Hungary. In 1878, his family left for the United States. They settled in Appleton, Wisconsin.

ASIA
EUROPE
Hungary
AFRICA

The Magic Begins

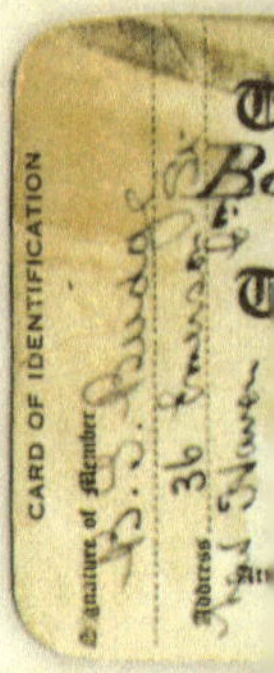

In 1887, the family moved to New York City, New York. Later, Erik and his friend Jacob started a magic act. They called themselves "The Brothers Houdini." Erik went by Harry Houdini.

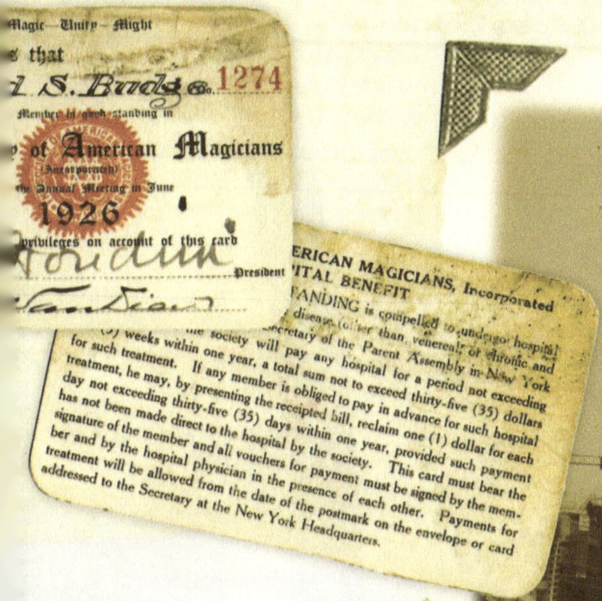

Magic—Unity—Might
s that
1274
Member in good standing in
of American Magicians
(Incorporated)
the Annual Meeting in June
1926
privileges on account of this card
President
ERICAN MAGICIANS, Incorporated
ITAL BENEFIT
TANDING is compelled to undergo hospital
disease (other than venereal, or chronic and
Secretary of the Parent Assembly in New York
the society will pay any hospital for a period not exceeding
(5) weeks within one year, a total sum not to exceed thirty-five (35) dollars
for such treatment. If any member is obliged to pay in advance for such hospital
treatment, he may, by presenting the receipted bill, reclaim one (1) dollar for each
day not exceeding thirty-five (35) days within one year, provided such payment
has not been made direct to the hospital by the society. This card must bear the
signature of the member and all vouchers for payment must be signed by the member and by the hospital physician in the presence of each other. Payments for
treatment will be allowed from the date of the postmark on the envelope or card
addressed to the Secretary at the New York Headquarters.

In 1893, Jacob left the act. Harry met a girl named Bess. The two married. Bess also joined the act. Together, they were "The Houdinis."

ARRY
THE
HOUDINIS
BESSI
INTRODUCING
THE ONLY AND ORIGINAL
METAMORPHOSIS

In 1899, Houdini performed his handcuff act in St. Paul, MN. A theater manager was watching. He set the Houdinis up for shows around the country.

In 1907, Harry performed his bridge jump. Cuffed and chained, he jumped into water. He freed himself and swam to the surface. It was unsafe. But people believed they had seen magic.

In 1912, Harry debuted the underwater box escape. By 1918, he had perfected another trick. He made an elephant disappear!

Hollywood

Harry's popularity caught Hollywood's attention. He starred in his first motion picture in 1918. It was called *The Master Mystery*.

B. A. ROLFE PRODUCTIONS

OCTAGON FILMS, INC.

HOUDINI

IN

The Master Mystery

A Super - Serial in Fifteen Episodes

EPISODE TWELVE

"The Death Noose"

B. A. ROLFE PRODUCTIONS

Harry did many stunts in his movies. People loved it. Now he was known for more than just magic.

Death & Legacy

In 1926, Harry died on Halloween in Detroit, MI. He is remembered as a great entertainer.

Timeline

1874 — **March 24**
Erik Weisz is born in Budapest, Hungary.

1878 — Erik and his family move to Appleton, Wisconsin, in the United States.

1887 — Erik and his family move to New York City, New York.

1891 — A theater manager sees the Houdinis perform in St. Paul, MN, and sets them up for shows across the country.

1893 — Harry marries Bess. Bess joins the act. The two are called The Houdinis.

1899 — A theater manager sees the Houdinis perform in St. Paul, MN, and sets them up for shows across the country.

1907 — Houdini performs his first bridge jump in Rochester, New York.

1918 — Houdini stars in *The Master Mystery*, his first motion picture.

1926 — **October 31**
Houdini dies in Detroit, MI.

Glossary

debut – the first public appearance.

popularity – the favor of the general public.

stunt – a performance showing a person's athletic skill.

surface – just above water.

Rosa Parks

Activist for Equality

by Grace Hansen

Photo Credits: AP Images, Corbis, Getty Images, iStock, Library of Congress, Shutterstock

Production Contributors: Teddy Borth, Jennie Forsberg, Grace Hansen
Design Contributors: Laura Mitchell, Dorothy Toth

Table of Contents

Birth & Early Life

Rosa McCauley was born on February 4, 1913. She was born in Tuskegee, Alabama.

Alabama

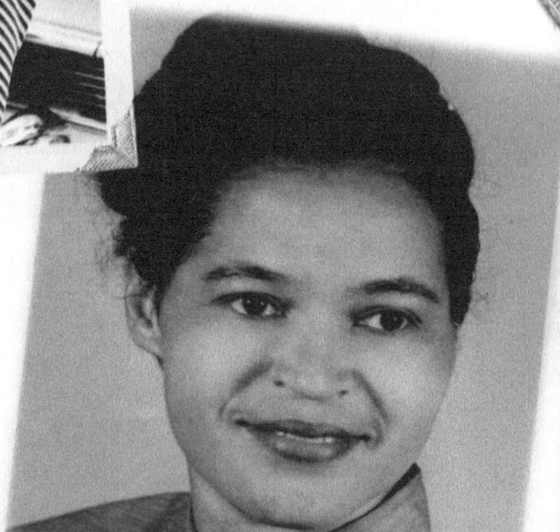

Rosa and her family moved to Montgomery, Alabama. The city had Jim Crow laws. These laws separated blacks and whites.

I CANT GO TO
SCHOOL BECAUSE
OF
SEGREGATION.
PLAY

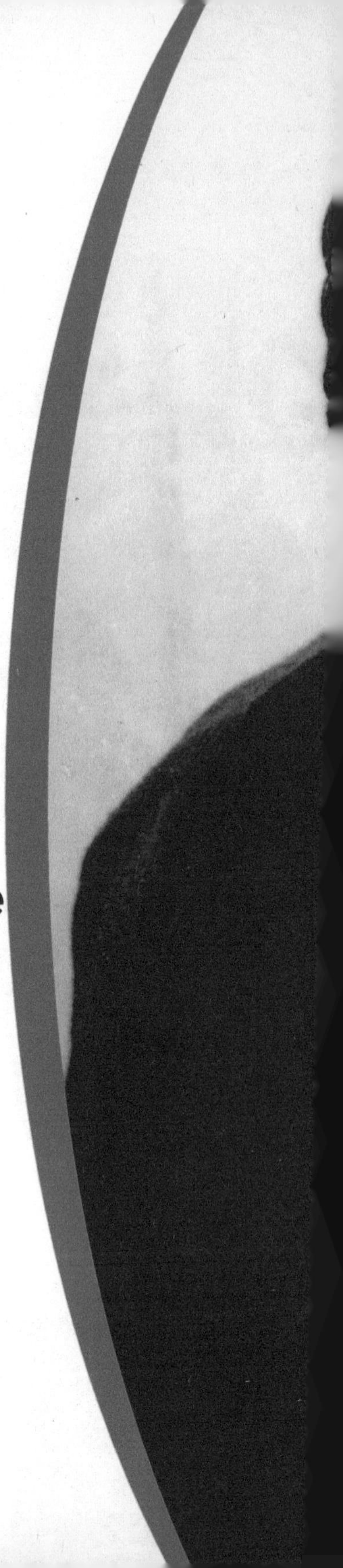

At 19, Rosa married Raymond Parks. He was a barber. Rosa was a seamstress. But she wanted to do more. She joined the NAACP in 1943.

The Bus

On December 1, 1955, Rosa got on the bus. She sat in the section for blacks. The seats for whites were full. The driver told Rosa to move to make more room.

Rosa refused to move. She was tired of the unfair laws. She was put in jail.

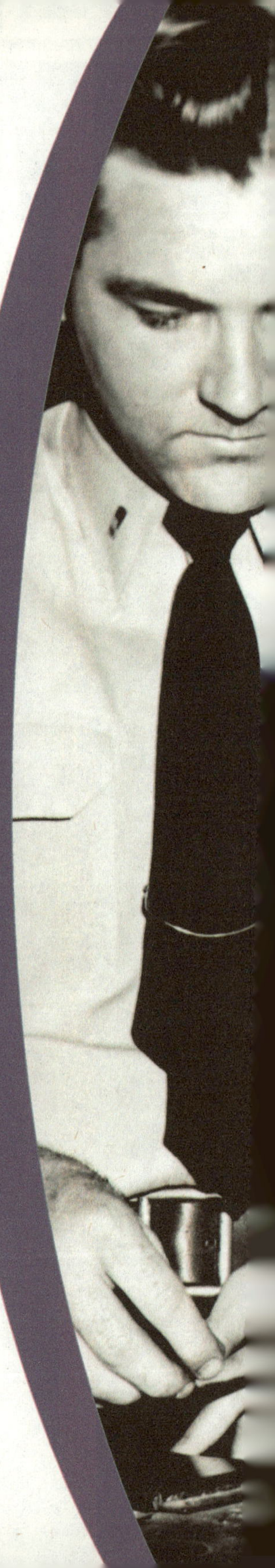

Change

On December 5, Rosa went to trial. The NAACP planned a boycott on the same day. No black person would ride the buses until laws changed.

On November 13, 1956, the Supreme Court ruled. It said that segregation was unfair. The boycott ended on December 20.

WATCH YOUR STEP

Laws changed in Montgomery. But racism was still there. The Parkses moved to Detroit, Michigan. They were happy there.

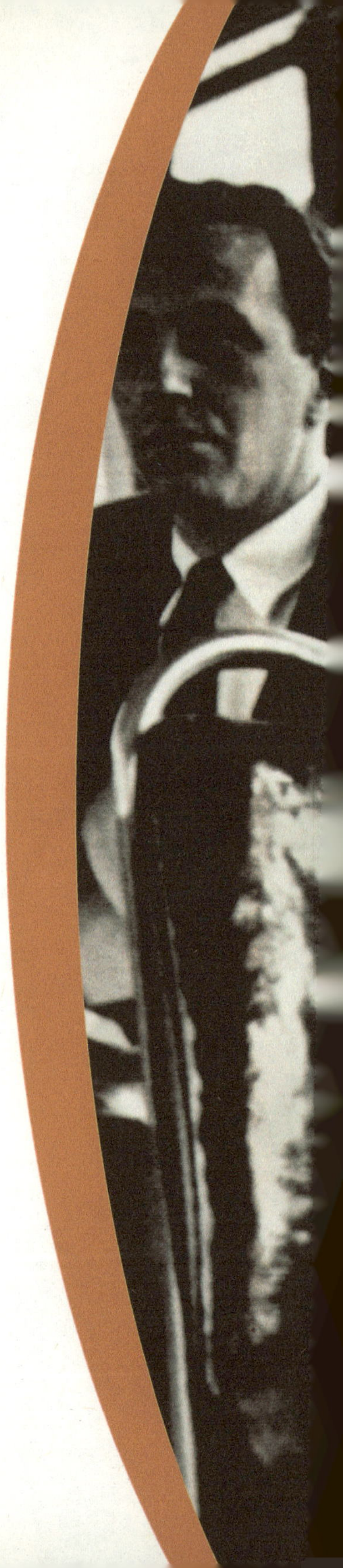

Death & Legacy

Rosa died on October 24, 2005. She proved that a small act could make a big change.

Timeline

1913 **February 4**
Rosa Louise McCauley is born in Tuskegee, Alabama.

1932 Rosa marries Raymond Parks. A year later, she graduates high school.

1943 Rosa joins the NAACP as a youth leader and secretary.

1955 **December 1**
Rosa is arrested when she refuses to give up her seat to white passengers on a bus.

December 5
Rosa goes to trial. The NAACP begins the Montgomery Bus Boycott.

1956 **November 13**
The Supreme Court rules that Jim Crow laws are unfair.

December 20
The bus boycott officially ends.

1987 **October 23**
Rosa dies at the age of 92.

2005 The Rosa and Raymond Parks Institute for Self-Development is founded.

Glossary

boycott - an act of joining with others to ban a certain person, product, place, or organization.

Jim Crow laws - state and local laws that made racial segregation legal in the Southern United States.

NAACP - stands for the National Association for the Advancement of Colored People. The organization formed in 1909 to ensure equality of rights of all persons, and to end racism.

seamstress - a woman whose job is sewing.

segregation - the act of separating people based on gender, race, or something else. Jim Crow laws made this legal in the South.

Supreme Court - the highest court of a state or of the U.S.